Fair's Fair

Fair's Fair

by Leon Garfield
Illustrated by S. D. Schindler

DOUBLEDAY & COMPANY, INC. GARDEN CITY, NEW YORK

Designed by Marianne Bosshart

Text copyright © 1981 by Leon Garfield
Illustrations copyright © 1983 by S. D. Schindler

All Rights Reserved
Printed in the United States of America
First Edition

Library of Congress Cataloging in Publication Data
Garfield, Leon.
  Fair's fair.

  Summary: Two orphans are lured to an immense mansion by a
mysterious dog where, because of their compassion, hard work,
patience, and kindness, they make the transformation from rags
to riches.
    [1. Orphans—Fiction.   2. Christmas—Fiction]
I. Schindler, S. D., ill.   II. Title.
PZ7.G17943Fai   1983   [E]   81-43136
          ISBN: 0-385-17963-4 (prebound)
          ISBN: 0-385-17962-6 (trade)

JACKSON WAS THIN, small and ugly, and stank like a drain. He got his living by running errands, holding horses, and doing a bit of scrubbing on the side. And when he had nothing better to do he always sat on the same doorstep at the back of Paddy's Goose, which was at the worst end of the worst street in the worst part of the town. He was called Jackson, because his father might have been a sailor, Jack being a fond name for a sailor in the streets round Paddy's Goose; but nobody knew for sure. He had no mother, either, so there was none who would have missed him if he'd fallen down a hole in the road. And nobody *did* miss him when he vanished one day and was never seen or heard of again.

It happened when Christmas was coming on—about a week before. Dreadful weather, as hard and bitter as a quarrel. Dreadful weather, with snowflakes fighting in the wind and milk freezing in the pail.

Jackson was out in it, sitting on his doorstep with his hands cupped together just over his knees. There was a whisker of steam coming up from his mouth and another from between his hands. It wasn't his soul going up to heaven, it was a hot pie from a shop around the corner where he'd been scrubbing the kitchen since before it was light.

He couldn't make up his mind whether it was better to be warm outside or in. He couldn't make up his mind whether it would be better to keep the pie and warm his hands, or to eat it and warm his insides. So there he was, thinking hard, with his face screwed up like a piece of dirty paper, when the black dog came.

Huge: as big as a donkey, nearly, with eyes like streetlamps and jaws like an oven door. Down the street it padded, with a glare to the right and a glare to the left, and a savage twitch of its great black nose. Somebody opened a window and threw a bucket of dirty water down; and the black dog snarled with rage. Up it came to the doorstep where Jackson sat and steamed. It glared and growled while the snowflakes fried on his nose.

"Shove off!" wails Jackson, hiding his pie and shaking in his shoes—or, rather, in his feet as he had no shoes worth mentioning. "I got no food and I'm only skin and bone myself so I'll taste as sour as leaves!"

"Liar!" says the dog, not in words but with its terrible eyes and rattling teeth.

"I'm froze and hungry!" wails Jackson, wishing he'd eaten the pie.

"And *I'm* froze and hungry!" says the dog, not in words but with its lean sides and smoking breath.

"All right," says Jackson, seeing there's no sense in arguing. "Fair's fair. Half for you and half for me." And he breaks the pie and the dog swallows down half with a fearful guzzle and growl. "Fair's fair," says Jackson, and eats what's left. "Now shove off!"

But the black dog just stands and bangs at the falling snow with its tail. Then, big as the night, with its streetlamp eyes, it comes straight at Jackson; and licks his face. Not because it loves him, but because Jackson smells as much of pie as he does of drains.

"You're spifflicating me!" howls Jackson, and tries to push the monster off. He gets his hands round its tree of a neck and then cries out, "Hullo! You got a collar on! You must belong to somebody. Hullo again! You got something under your collar. What you got? Stone the crows! You got a key!"

Sure enough, it's an iron key, heavy enough to open a church. Jackson stares at it, stares at the monstrous dog, stares at the monstrous weather. Snow coming down in dirty fistfuls and not a soul in sight. Not a horse to be held, not an errand to be run, and his knuckles still raw from his last scrubbing.

"Seeing as how," says Jackson to the monster, "I got time on me hands and no business in view, I'll spare you an hour and take you home. All we got to do is to find the door this key will fit. Shouldn't be hard."

So up he gets; and that was the last that was seen of Jackson, and of the black dog down Bluegate way. Nobody knew for sure whether the great black dog had swallowed up Jackson, or Jackson had swallowed up the dog; and the wild white snow swallowed up whichever one of them was left.

"All we got to do," says Jackson, "is to find the right door. Shouldn't be hard," he said, as they went along the hundredth street. "There must be one somewhere with a hole that'll fit this key."

The doors he tried! Short fat doors with panels all over like a poacher's pockets; tall thin doors with iron studs down the middle, like a bishop's buttons; doors with little windows, doors with fan-lights, doors with pillars, doors with porches, doors with horrible knockers and doors with brass letter boxes that had eyes inside them when you looked through. And gates! Gates with mansions inside, gates with churches inside, gates with prisons inside, gates with graveyards inside and gates with nothing at all inside.

"Fair's fair!" sighed Jackson, as he tramped on, with the key in front of him and the huge black dog behind. "There must be a door somewhere with a hole to fit this key!"

But there wasn't; even though he trudged every street, every lane, every avenue, every square, mews, alley and court. Nothing. And the worst of it was that the snow kept coming down on tiptoe and craftily muffling where he'd been, so he never knew if he'd gone down that street before.

"I'll be an old man," groaned Jackson, "before I'm done; and you'll be an old dog. There must be more houses with more doors than you and me's got minutes left to go. So fair's fair. You take a turn at it."

"All right," said the dog, not in words but with a terrible gape of its terrible jaws.

Jackson put the key inside and the jaws clamped shut, and the black monster padded away to the north.

Jackson went after, and, while the sky grew darker and the town grew whiter, they tramped and tramped in search of a door with a hole to fit the key. At last they came up on top of Hampstead Heath, where ghostly houses twinkled among ghostly trees, and ghostly coaches with tall white hats rolled silently by. The monster began to whine and snarl and growl.

"Fair's fair," said Jackson. "I'm frightened too. But I ain't complaining. I'm tired too. But I ain't sitting down in the snow. Come on with you! There must be a house with a door with a hole that'll fit this key!"

But the dog wouldn't move. It dropped the key and Jackson had to pick it up before it vanished into the snow. He looked about him. Hard to tell if they were on a road or a frozen river. Hard to tell if that was a gate and a path or the beginning of a forest.

It was a gate. Jackson went through, and so did the huge black dog. There was a house among trees, bulging with chimneys and turrets and looking like three houses that had climbed on top of each other. Not a light in it, not a glimmer, not a twinkle, even. An old dead house with an old dead door, with an iron letter box as thin as a miser's mouth.

Jackson said, "I hope this ain't the one."

But it was. The key fitted and turned in the lock.

"Fair's fair," said Jackson. "You go first. You're bigger than me."

There was a candle burning on a table in the hall, and a smell of onions, gravy and roast beef.

"Anybody home?" called Jackson, up a grand staircase that lost itself in shadows.

"Home!" came down an echo. "Home—home—home!"

"I brung back your dog!"

"Dog—dog—dog!"

"I got to be going now!"

"Now—now—now!"

"Well," said Jackson. "Somebody must be about. Somebody must have lit the candle. Maybe they've fallen asleep."

He began to look, first in one room, then in another, then in another. They were all dark and nobody answered when he called. He went upstairs, and the dog followed after, growling and whining all the way. There was a glimmer of light coming from under a door. Jackson knocked. No answer. He called. No answer. He turned the handle and went inside.

What a room! As long as a street, nearly, and tall and wide to match! Candles in silver candlesticks, pictures in gold frames, china plates on a shining table, roast beef on a sideboard and a roaring fire in the grate! What a room! And there in a chair big enough for six, at the head of the table, with a knife, fork and munching mouth, sat a small, thin, dirty, tattered, angry little girl!

"I brung back your dog," said Jackson, "miss."

She finished up what she was eating and put down her knife and fork.

"Not my dog," said she. "Too big, too black and too hungry for me."

"He had your key," said Jackson, eyeing the roast beef and watching the gravy. "Under his collar, miss."

"Not my key," said she. "Key of the house, that's all."

"Not your house then? How did you come here?"

"How did *you* come here?"

Jackson told her.

"Same like me," she said. "Day before yesterday, just after dark."

"And you're still here?"

"That's right. It were late when me and the dog came, so I slept in a chair downstairs, big enough for six. In the morning there was eggs, butter, milk and bread left just inside the door. So me and the dog had breakfast; then we had dinner; then we had supper, just like a queen and king. And since then, every time I've nodded off, there's been something left to eat, just inside the door."

Jackson nodded. "Fair's fair," he said. "It must be because you
brung back their dog. Mind if I sit down and have a bite?"

"Fair's fair," said the girl. "You brung back the dog, too.."

"What's your name?" asked Jackson, sharing some beef with
the dog.

"They call me Lillipolly, down Shadwell way. What's yours?"

"They call me Jackson, down Bluegate way."

"I cleaned all the silver and polished the table," said Lillipolly,
"so it'll be nice for 'em when they come home."

"Fair's fair," said Jackson. "I'll do the grate and the kitchen
floor."

"I wonder," said Lillipolly, "if it's really a dog! I wonder if it's
him what does it all the time? I wonder if he changes into something
else, like a prince, when I'm not looking, and brings the food and
leaves it by the door?"

"Shouldn't think so," said Jackson. "But let's take it in turns to
watch and see."

Down the stairs they went and took a candle into the room where the armchairs were big enough for six. They settled themselves down and the dog lay in front of the wide dark fireplace and heaved a growling sigh. Lillipolly took the first watch; Jackson took the second, and the dog took the third as Jackson and Lillipolly were fast asleep.

In the morning, just as Lillipolly had said, milk, butter, eggs and bread were left on a tray inside the door.

"It *must* be him," said Lillipolly, pointing to the dog. "He must have turned into something while we was asleep."

"I don't see," said Jackson, "how he could have turned into anything except another sort of dog."

After breakfast Lillipolly swept the stairs and polished the bannisters while Jackson washed the dishes and fetched the coal. The dog did nothing at all.

"Fair's fair," said Jackson. "He's only a dog after all."

"Do you think," said Lillipolly, "they'll come home for Christmas?"

"Everybody comes home for Christmas," said Jackson. "Or so they say."

But the days went by and nobody came, save a duck, a goose and a roasted chicken, on dishes inside the door; until at last it was Christmas Eve.

"It must be a dream," said Jackson, "and I'll wake up and be on me doorstep again, back of Paddy's Goose. But let's keep on dreaming, and, seeing how things has been I shouldn't be surprised to find a roast turkey and a plum pudding twice as big as me head, just inside the door."

But Jackson *was* surprised, because there was nothing inside the door, not so much as an egg. So Jackson and Lillipolly went hungry, and the black dog went outside. Nothing came all that day, save once they were upstairs by the fire. Six mince pies in a silver dish lay steaming on the mat.

"We'll keep 'em hot in front of the fire," said Jackson, "and eat 'em when it gets dark."

They waited until the sky turned black and they could see their own faces looking back at them from the windows, like ghost children in the air.

"Time for pies," said Jackson.

"Look!" said Lillipolly. "Look what's coming through the gate!"

Six small children, smaller even than Jackson and Lillipolly, with lanterns to light their faces, came and stood outside in the freezing snow. Then six small mouths opened and carols came floating up. Herald Angels, Merry Gentlemen and Good King Wenceslas and all. Then came a knock on the door. Jackson went down and opened it.

"Merry Christmas!" sang the children in the snow.

"Fair's fair!" called Jackson up to Lillipolly. "They're cold and we're warm, so let's give 'em the pies!"

So up he went and came down with Lillipolly and the pies.

"Merry Christmas!" they said to the small singers, and watched them go off munching the hot mince pies. Then they went into the room downstairs, meaning to go to sleep.

Two men were standing there, waiting for them! Two ragged, fearful, old and wild-looking men! Two men who must have crept in while they'd been fetching the pies.

"Where's your father and mother?" growled one in a terrible voice.

"Don't know," said Jackson.

"And never did," said Lillipolly. "What are you doing here?"

"None of your business," growled the other man, and bared his teeth like a hungry wolf.

"There's silver here," said the first.

"And pictures," said the second, "and brass and fine china plates."

"We'll take it all," said the first man, with a greedy snarl.

"Fair's fair," said Jackson. "There's a fire to get warm by; there's a roof to keep off the snow; and there's chairs down here to sleep in, big enough for six. Ain't that enough?"

"Fair's fair," said Lillipolly. "They'll be coming home for Christmas, and I got everything clean and nice."

"Who's they? Who'll be coming home for Christmas?" asked the first man.

"Them what lives in this house," said Jackson and Lillipolly together.

The two men looked at each other; then the first one clapped his hands.

He took off his ragged coat and underneath was a handsome suit of clothes, with a gold watch chain, and in all likelihood, a gold watch too. The other man did the same, and two fine gentlemen stood before Jackson and Lillipolly, smiling and nodding their heads.

"My name," said the first one, "is Mr. Beecham Chamber; and this is my lawyer, Mr. Chuter & Ede."

"I'm Jackson," said Jackson. "And she's Lillipolly, who got here before me by two days. We brung back your dog. We'll be going now, if you like."

"You can stay, if you like."

"For Christmas?"

"Forever, if you like."

"Fair's fair. We only brung back your dog."

"Fair's fair," said Mr. Beecham Chambers. "You've done much more than that. You see, I'm a lonely old man, so I asked Mr. Chuter & Ede if he could find two children, who had no homes, who would come and live with me and be as my own. I asked Mr. Chuter & Ede if he could find two children who were kind, who were brave, who were patient, who were honest and who were generous. Mr. Chuter & Ede said it was impossible. Two such children could never be found. But he was wrong. *I* found them with the help of Growler, my dog."

"How come?" asked Jackson and Lillipolly together.

Mr. Beecham Chambers smiled. "Both of you," he said, "must have been kind to have fed Growler; both of you must have been brave to have taken his key. Both of you must have been patient to have found this house; both of you must have been honest for you've stayed and stolen nothing away; and both of you must have been generous to have given away your last six pies.

"There now, Mr. Chuter & Ede," said Mr. Beecham Chambers to his lawyer, "have I not done the impossible? Have I not found, with the help of Growler, the two very children I dreamed of?"

"You have indeed," said Mr. Chuter & Ede. "But they are two in a million, I can tell you. Or even in ten million, I shouldn't be surprised."

"Fair's fair," said Jackson, with his arm round Lillipolly to make sure he was awake. "Anybody would have done the same!"

So that's what really happened to Jackson, and to Lillipolly as well. And you may look as hard and as long as you like round the back of Paddy's Goose and round Shadwell way; and you won't see either of them there again.